Positive Psyhology:

Manage Your Negative Thinking And Stop Programming Yourself To A Failure

Table of content

Introduction

Although humans share a common physical frame with common body parts yet on the basis of psychology every individual is a unique entity. The interplay of psychological and cognitive resources makes an exclusive connection and we see various effects of this psychological domain in various different phases of human life.

Just as human knowledge and wisdom has increased, a number of fruitful contributions have been made so that the general public and whole mankind can get benefit from these extended applications of this psychological knowledge. One of the most famous trends getting highlighted nowadays is the inclination of studying and diagnosing negative thoughts. Negative thoughts are truly harmful if left unattended. These can even present serious threats to the society because the survival of a society is based upon the mental and physical health of its citizens. So an overall treatment of negative thoughts is necessary for the survival of societies as well as individuals.

Negative thoughts are not essentially a matter of psychologist or therapist. Even with personal and individual efforts one can get positive results against these thoughts. The first step is to gain knowledge about these thoughts so that one can truly diagnose and then work for the positive treatment of these thoughts. This book will provide you the knowledge about the negative thoughts in the simplest way so that the applicability is made easier for everyone. The discussion is supported and enhanced by daily life examples so that understanding the complex interplay of negative thoughts is made easier.

Chapter 1 – The variable kinds of negative thinking- a diagnostic approach

The human psychology and thinking process is one of the most complex phenomenons. The different shades of human personality and connecting cognitive processes make human thinking a complex procedure. It is one of the deepest fields of studies which aim at understanding the different causes of variability, which is depicted across personalities and their attitudes.

Whether it is some academic research or medicinal research the human factor is the ultimate driving force. It calls for a need to investigate the true colors of human psychology.

One of the fundamental presumptions underlying the cognitive model and other psychology models is that the human thinking is governed by the feelings of a person. A same scenario can present different thinking, based on variable feelings. So thinking is not independent of feelings, moods and attitudes.

This variability in thoughts draws a distinction between the good times and bad times. There can be times when a person feels trapped in unconstructive and pointless thoughts. But merely knowing about the existence of this variation is not enough. Recognizing the negative thoughts and contextual factors which leads to these thoughts is crucial for effective management of negative thoughts.

The categories of negative thoughts

Although psychological distinctions are hard to be obvious yet negative thoughts can be categorized into following major divisions.

> ➤ **Overgeneralization**:

It refers to a category of negative thoughts which emerges when a person draws general conclusion referring to merely on a sole evidence or single event. Rather than refining the conclusions, the person just keeps in mind one incidence and thinks that it will exactly happen in the same way again and again. These thoughts usually accompany extreme negative and collective phrases like "never" and "always".

E.g. "My presentation did not go well today. I can never do it right"

"My husband left me alone. Men are always like this".

> ➤ **Filtering or Selective Abstraction:**

It can better be said to as selective filtering with a negative valence. In this case the person focuses on the negatives while positive aspects are ignored. It eventually leads to the eradication of important cognitive information that pertains to positive aspects. So a selective view based on negative abstraction emerges.

E.g. "he (my manager) said most of my report was good but he also stated there were various highlighted mistakes which need correction. He must be thinking of me as purely hopeless"

> ➤ **Dichotomous Reasoning:**

It is like an all or nothing approach which makes decision either in black or in white. It makes the person to think of a phenomenon either wrong or right, bad or good. The person lacks the middle approach, only the two valences are thought of.

E.g. "This place is so terrible, nothing is good here". "I will not be able to finish this task, so I should not start it".

In this way the person while being in search of "everything" remains devoid of even "something".

> **Undue Personalizing:**

These are the type of negative thoughts which make the person think that he is responsible for an event or incidence (mostly disastrous or catastrophic). They blame themselves for being responsibility for an event, whereas in reality there is nothing as their fault. Even they mold the words or reactions of people considering them as being directed towards their personality.

E.g. *"Daddy is in an awful mood. Surely I would have done something wrong".*

"I know she never liked me, otherwise she could not ignore me saying a hello".

> **Catastrophising:**

It is the negative thinking which drives a person to think that the chances of facing a disaster or catastrophe higher. These people overestimate the possibility of disaster and never expect something positive to happen. It eventually makes them get unconfident and they think that they will not be able to handle any situation and ultimately disaster will be their destiny.

E.g. *I'm going to look clumsy and all friends will poke at me.*

If I don't present well today, my boss will get me terminated.

➤ **Emotional Reasoning:**

These negative thoughts place a veil of mistaken feelings over the real facts. In this way negative feelings about one's self are supposed to be true because they are affirmed by an internal set of feelings.

E.g. "I have a gut feeling for failure, I know I will fail".

"I always feel ugly in front of him; hence I ought to be ugly".

"I feel very hopeless in front of him, so my situation is ought to be hopeless".

➤ **Mind Reading:**

The people driven by these kinds of negative feelings lack the ability to check the evidence and make assumptions regarding the thoughts, behaviors and feelings of other people. They lack the ability of rationale thinking and logical reasoning.

E.g. "Cathy is talking to Tom, so she must have a more liking for him".

"I know he will refuse my invitation, he is least interested in me".

➤ **Fortune Telling Error:**

The people under this negative thought start behaving like fortune tellers. They have a greater tendency to ignore the facts and realities and base their anticipations on their personal assumptions. As they believe on negative assumptions so they act accordingly an in most cases the expectations are fulfilled which make them more confident about their fortune telling capability. As a vicious cycle the chances of getting changed are largely reduced.

E.g. "he has always been a cheater, he will also cheat you this time".

"This ATM machine never works out so it is not wise to waste my time here".

"This company will surely get bankrupted".

➤ Should Statements:

Negative thoughts can make a person believe on internal feelings, gut instincts and assumptions, so he or she frequently uses the words like "ought", "should", and "must" in their statements. It leads to a set up of unrealistic expectations about one's own self as well as about others. These negative thoughts operate by rigid rules and with the absence of any kind of flexibility.

E.g. *"I shouldn't trust him".*

"She should be kind to me every time"

➤ Magnification or Minimization:

These people have the tendency to over emphasize the significance of negative experiences or information, while reducing or even ignoring the positive experiences or information.

E.g. "He saw that I spilled drink over my shirt. I know he will take me along with him again".

"Supporting her on the death of his mother still doesn't make up for that time; I got angry at her last year".

Knowing about these different types of negative thoughts and your tendency to exhibit these thought at different occasions can help you to consciously work against these. The eventual happiness of your life rests with a need to eradicate negative thoughts; otherwise the whole life can get a negative orientation.

Chapter 2 – The Connections of Labeling Technique with Negative Thoughts

Nothing takes place in isolation, neither the thoughts nor the actions. Same is the case with negative thoughts. They do not take place in isolation. One such connecting phenomenon, which triggers the promotion of negative thoughts in a person, is the "labeling process". It describes the interaction phenomenon of behaviors and thoughts.

The "labeling" technique
The labeling technique is a part of our daily life. It is rather an unconscious part of our life. Every day we apply labels to people, groups and incidences. Some of our fellows are labeled as "smart" by constantly being exposed to appraisal statements like:

"Wow, you are really intelligent. You always prove to be the winner".

Unluckily, there are also labels such as "dumb", which connote statements like:

"You are such a goof! You can never prove yourself to be capable of doing anything".

The biggest mystery lies in the fact that both these labeling prove out to be correct and these people behave as per the expectations. So the biggest question arises that are our predications good enough for human behaviors? Or it is the labeling which is the root cause of a particular type of behavior.

Labeling influences behaviors:
There have been many different researches which came out with the results that behaviors are driven by a particular type of label.

One of the most prominent experiments was the one which was conducted in USA. The citizens were randomly labeled "good citizens" and "average citizens" and were asked about voting tendency. The labeling was purely based on random sampling but on actual voting day the people who were labeled good citizens were having 15% greater rates of voting. Hence it proved that labeling endorses specific behaviors.

This topic is greatly focused in child and education studies where a child can be molded in a particular way by using specific labels.

Limiting labels:
These labels actually act at the level of performance and behaviors. Negative thinking is largely driven by these limiting labels. These can be applied on others as well as on one's self.

On others

This has reflective consequences in the day to day life. For instance you are a teacher, and there is a student in your class who is not that brilliant or not doing well in class. Now if you become furious and state the labeled phrases like, "You can never work! You will never be able to do anything well", you have unconsciously labeled the student as "indolent" and "unable." Eventually the student will see his or her personality through the lens of the labels which you stated. He will act in the same manner, over and over again.

Alternatively, if you are really interested to motivate this student, you have to make use of labels which state the potentials of that student. The encouragement labels can help him to explore his potentials. Use labels which prove to be positive and encouraging: "I see so much potential in you to prove high achievements, I can assure that if you work hard a little you can be much better." Eventually the student will confine to your expectations.

On yourself

The use of labels is not confined to others only. Many of the times people use labels for themselves also. We frequently come across thoughts which push us to say, "I am too bad at mathematics."

This limiting label conveys a signal to our brain, enforcing it to act poorly during mathematical tasks. The brain also acts like a programming machine which follows the principle of "garbage in, garbage out". It will act as it is commanded and programmed by our own intuitions and labeling.

This labeling can provide far off consequences in our life. If you label yourself like "I can never be a good spokesman", it will always get in front of you during each public gathering and you will feel unconfident and nervous. So limiting labels can make you devoid of many bright opportunities in life.

Labels are not irreversible
One of the good things about these labels is that they are under our control and they can be changed through conscious and deliberate efforts.

Steps involved in changing the labels:

1. Acknowledgment of the problem:

Many of our problems prevail because we remain unaware or ignorant. During first step of changing the limiting labels, you have to acknowledge that there is a problem created by a specific label. Moreover, only one label at a time should be handled, otherwise things can get complicated.

2. Determine the cost incurred:

Once you have identified the problematic label, the next step is to analyze the cost which you are bearing because of this label. Determine the opportunities which you could not avail because of the label and what those opportunities meant to you?

3. Make a Conscious choice

In your mind make up a firm view that you want to change this label and you will make deliberate efforts for it.

4. Replace the limiting one with an empowering one

Choose another label which can be more empowering than the limiting label. Consciously put efforts for crafting a good label.

5. Use of transition labels

The brain takes some time in getting used to new routines; same is the case with the use of labels. Initially when you will use a new label the brain may get some time in accepting it. So it is more realistic to use some transition label. For example you may replace a limiting label like "I am always nervous" with "I can be confident". But a better approach is to use a transition label like, "I am becoming good in confidence day by day". The brain will better respond to this realistic approach.

6. Take actions

Now when you have taken the transition label, the next step is to put this label into action by acting accordingly. In case of confidence labels described above, start acting confidently. The initial few attempts may not be ideal but trying for it will mean that you are conforming to the transition labels.

7. Go out of comfort zone

For changing the labels and consequent actions, you have to live out of your comfort zone. You have to get out of your usual inclinations and make deliberate efforts.

8. remain persistent

While struggling for this change of labels and resulting behaviors you have to remain firm and persistent. Continuity will make better results, rather than just using the same old routines. Labels will not work in this case so you have to prove them with accurate actions.

Chapter 3 – Cognitive connections of emotions and situations

Whether we observe it consciously or not, but our brain is at a constant working mode. Even when we are sleeping, some part of our mind is awake and performing various cognitive processes, including dreaming. When we talk about thoughts and especially negative thoughts the role of brain becomes even more significant. Our brain is continuously exposed to object, events and labeling. From simple matters like what to eat and what to cook for today, to the more complex decisions like which career to pursue, all are thought upon through your brain. So you can see the limitless burden over this part of body.

When even a machine is exposed to so much work pressures, the chances of wear and tear are enhanced. So is the case with brain. It can deviate from healthy and optimum working. Psychologists believe that negative thoughts cannot be stated as a malfunctioning of a brain. In fact these thinking patterns are connected to many other factors.

Cognitive approach of thinking and emotions:

A potential question to ask is the causal connection between situations and emotions. It is a proven reality that emotions are governed by a particular situation. Situations and events have the potential to change the emotions in no time.

Another recent advance in the field of personality and human psychology is that even the thoughts are the predictors of emotions. So the effect of situations on emotions is only half of the story, the remaining half is the way in which a person interprets the situation and event. Together these two factors make up the ultimate effect on emotions. The beliefs, thoughts and perception put effect on emotions.

Based on this phenomenal finding the psychologists are now able to deal with different problems through cognitive therapy. One of which is the treatment of negative thoughts.

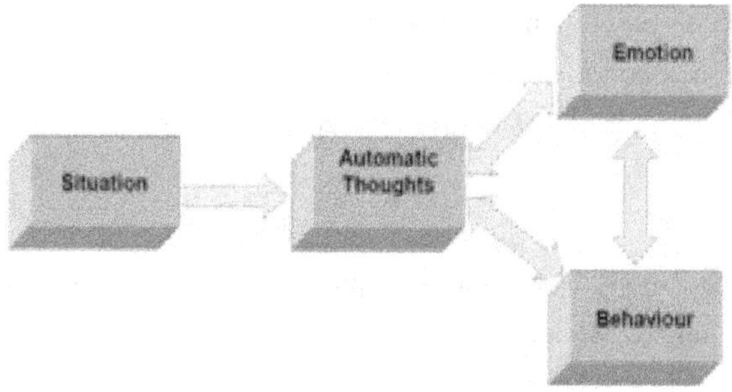

This model explains the eventual connection which is focused during the cognitive therapy.

We can explain this model with an example in which the situation remains the same but variable thoughts can produce variable emotions.

Situation	Thought	Resulting Emotion
A friend is late for the Theatre.	I hope she is all right, nothing bad happened to her	anxiety

A friend is late for the Theatre.	He is never on time	anger
A friend is late for the Theater.	I knew she do not like me and do not want to spend time with me	sadness

The column labeled here as thoughts can be clearer if we label it as "**Automatic thought**". It refers to sensations, images, memories or mental pictures which pass along the mind. These can be labeled as 'automatic' as they pass along quickly through our brain even when do not exactly know about them. These can be regarded as mental reflexes of our brain. In order to treat the negative thoughts there is an intense need to understand these automatic thoughts and the way they perform cognitive tasks. Although you are not fully aware of the way they occur in your brain yet a conscious effort can be made to treat these automatic thoughts.

The thinking traps

The researchers have explored common phenomenon known as 'cognitive Traps' or 'cognitive errors'. All types of distasteful emotions like sadness, anxiety or anger affect how we see the outer world. It is a kind of coloring to the outer world, which makes use of automatic thoughts only by filtering out of disconfirming verifications.

When you will consciously put efforts to eradicate a particular negative though, you will come to know that how irrational were you in seeing a particular phenomenon. When you will get away with negative thoughts you can see more logical and persuasive opinion, which was kept under the burden of negative thoughts. So if a particular situation triggers anxiety or sadness in you, it may be the result of overlooking the realities.

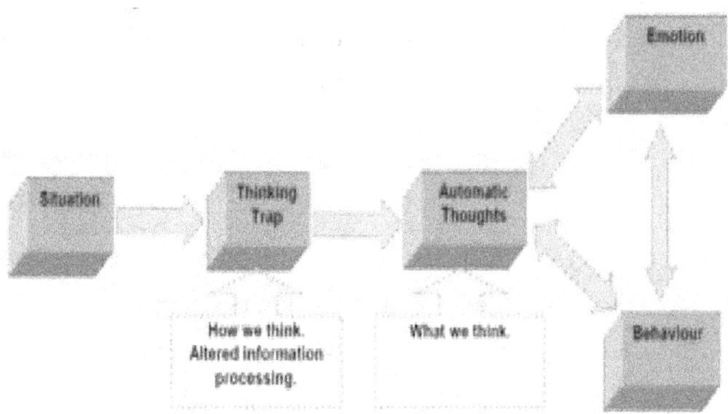

The model depicts the interplay of this cognitive trap. It is because of this reason that some people only notice or remember negative perceptions about a person, situation or experience. Similarly others are more inclined towards the positive valence. But the good thing is that you can work on these negative thoughts and thinking trap to ease your life and mental state as well as that of other people living around you.

The self fulfilling prophecy of negative talk:
One of the greatest traps for those who are indulged in negative self talk is the self fulfilling prophecy. They keep on adding negative views and thoughts in their mind and eventually these opinions thoughts and view stand in front of them like a reality. It is because they want to endorse their negative view or negative opinion and in that quest they start behaving or acting accordingly. This phenomenon is known as self fulfilling prophecy, in which a person behaves according to the widely held believes and views.

This self fulfilling prophecy can damage the person's personality as well as that of others. Their relationships can undergo turmoil or even their careers may suffer from hardships. It is because the stigma of being a negative actor sticks to them and they keep on adding to this by the vicious cycle of self fulfilling prophecy. One of the best ways to overcome it is to have a control over the thoughts which produce anxiety or depression. Try to think oppositely, this will be a conscious effort but once you will master this effort you will get to know its effectiveness within a short period of time.

Chapter 4 – Let us fight against the negative thoughts

Everyone wants to live a happy and contended life and everyone knows that negative thoughts are destructive. Still negative thoughts appear as a reality of life. When we talk about changing negative thoughts it does not connote to picture out the world in such a way that everything appears to be glowing and rosy. But the eventual rationale behind working against negative thoughts is to present a more objective, logical and realistic view of outside world and its events.

Life problems never get away by merely changing the thoughts. One common example is the situation when someone faces the death of his or her relatives or someone really close. Now in this case feeling sad, hopeless and painful is natural. None of the therapy can negate these thoughts. So the real objective is not aimed at putting these real feeling under the veil. But the objective is to know about these feelings so that one can cater them with a positive approach. It is essential because otherwise life will become really miserable and impossible to pass.

Cognitive restructuring

In a common language you may call it changing the negative thoughts but in psychological terms it is said to be cognitive restructuring or reappraising. Here are some methods and steps which we can follow while changing the course of thoughts.

Concentrate on your self-talk

Self-talk is a reality of every individual. It is a kind of inner dialogue, through which one says different things to one's own self, after facing a situation or event. The self talk lies in close proximity to the automatic thoughts and attitudes which result in specific emotions. The best possible way to deal with a negative or gloomy emotion is to start analyzing that what derived you to this emotion.

Some of the self dialogues which need your attention include:

- I'm a fool, a loser, a total collapse.

- I am sure this is out of my limits.

- I am losing my temper.

- I feel like fading.

- He is always intended to put me down.

- He does not love me.

- My colleagues will laugh at me.

Highlight the most recurrent thoughts

Try to figure out the thought which mostly leads to the same kind of emotion. Take the example that you had an argument at office, with your boss. Now you are feeling anxious. Below are the possibilities of thoughts which can come along your mind.

- He is a real brainless.

- He will terminate me.

- I wish I can say him what I wanted.

Now try to figure out the "hot thought", the one that can be the cause of highest levels of anxiousness. In many cases it will be the fear of getting fired.

Face up to the negative thoughts

Now try to figure out the realistic evidence from the hot thought, both in favor of it as well as against it. Now have a deeper view. Can you see the condition in another way? It can be very helpful for working against the thinking trap.

Rate your feelings:

Now try to figure out that does emotion decreased in its intensity? Can you notice the appearance of any positive emotion, such as reprieve, after getting away with negative thoughts? Carry a cue card along so that you may write it down. It can enhance the intensity of progress.

Thoughts feelings and physiology

Suppose you are said to make two sketches, one of a person who is sad and the other one who is happy. Most of the people think of a happy person as someone with a smile and good attentive attire. While the other one said to be sad, will be having disturbed attire.

This led the psychologist to think about the connections of physiology and thoughts. In the beginning it was supposed that the general mood or thoughts effect the person's attrite and physiology, as being in a bad mood makes a person disinterested in dressing up or making over. The relationship earlier maintained was:

Thoughts >> Feelings >> Physiology

But in the recent times, the researchers have explained another connection of relationship which exists between the same variables.

Physiology >> Feelings >> Thoughts

This relationship explains the power of body language and physiology. When the physiological signals send a gloomy message the person get trapped in the outlook problem, it will lead more firm way towards the negative thoughts. In this case the in confidence is added because of the bad attire can further enhance the negative thoughts. One cannot ignore the effectiveness and impression of physiology.

If you are determined to achieve positive thoughts start with connotation of positive dialogue accompanied with positive attire. Dress up well. Maintain good hygiene level especially the oral hygiene and eventually you will get up as a stronger and more confident person. It is one of the easiest ways to get across the negative thoughts with least effort.

For example on a day you are wearing very dull and bad dress. On the same day you are called for a presentation. You are also inclined to use limiting label that "I am bad at presenting proposals". Now this label will be reconfirmed by your poor attire because in presentations usually involve a confident body language. So in this case the physiology had been a great source in further enhancing the negative thoughts. If you had been in good attire, you could try with a positive thought but here the chance is completely diminished.

Some general tips for overcoming negative thoughts

➢ Practice is the best key to attain maximum achievement against negative thoughts, so do not quit practicing.

➢ Consider that automatic thoughts as your reflexes so do not get over conscious about the automatic thoughts. Provide yourself with 'free passes for automatic thoughts. This will save the undue wastage of energy.teh crystal point is to know about their existence and dealing with them with a constructive approach.

➢ Never struggle for all or nothing approach. It means never expect that the negative thoughts will diminish to zero percent. Even if it is declining with the passage of time it means you are making a progress. Do not loose energy and hope in eradicating the negative thoughts to zero level.

➢ On way to deal with negative thoughts is a try to follow a realistic rationale. Never indulge in presenting with unrealistic goals which are hard to achieve. The psychological goals are hardest of all to achieve.

➤ Do not believe on Automatic thoughts as truths. Deal with counterfactuals and have a firm belief that not all automatic thoughts are supposed to be true.

➤ Try to work out on the most frequent limiting labels which you choose. When a frequent one will be treated you will find much relief, as a larger part of the problem will be solved. Try to treat those labeling traps first, which cause the greatest problem for you. This approach from ascending to descending will keep you motivated for further progress.

➤ Although all thoughts need to be handled with care but figure out the hot thoughts first. It is possible when you achieve ability to list down the possible alternatives of negative thoughts and then distinguishing the hot thoughts.

Working on negative thoughts can be crucial in the start but once you start it you will really cherish the results.

Conclusion

Among all the creations extended by nature, we humans are the best and most complex one. Not only the physical systems of the body are coordinated and well managed but the psychological systems of human body is also one of the miracles. Since the very inception of medical and psychological field, the human psychology presents the most attractive topic.

Not only the psychological research is helpful in the field of academics but the applied psychology is also helping a number of people all around the world. One such topic under extensive application today is negative thoughts. It is because the effects of these thoughts are far flung. They can even govern the overall quality of life. The way a person faces the life and uses different cognitive approaches are very well catered under the discussion of negative thoughts. This topic is getting serious attention in various circles.

In this book we have tried to present a fruitful discussion about negative thoughts. The discussion has been extended at the most basic level so that you can easily apply this discussion and therapeutic suggestions in your daily life. Negative thoughts can prove to be destructive even at the societal level as well as at the individual level. We have therefore provided a collective approach for defining negative thoughts and various ways in which the thoughts can be catered. When you apply these methods regularly you will feel a clear change in the overall quality of your life and the level of happiness attained.

www.ingramcontent.com/pod-product-compliance
Lightning Source LLC
Chambersburg PA
CBHW070024260726
48658CB00003B/1020